# Interview with a TIGER
## with a
## & other clawed beasts too

Written by
Andy Seed

Illustrated by
Nick East

Published in 2020 by Welbeck Children's Books
An imprint of Welbeck Children's Limited, part of Welbeck Publishing Group.
20 Mortimer Street London W1T 3JW

Text © Andy Seed 2020
Illustrations © Nick East 2020

Design Manager: Emily Clarke
Associate Publisher: Laura Knowles
Editor: Jenni Lazell

ISBN 978-1-78312-647-7

Printed in Heshan, China

10 9 8 7 6 5 4 3

# Contents

# Introduction

What is a tiger's perfect day? What's not good about being a wolf? Do lions ever go to the movies? No, I'd never thought about these questions, either! But if you want to know the answers, you have the RIGHT BOOK.

I have been lucky—or unlucky—enough to sit down with ten BIG SCARY BEASTS with CLAWS and ask them questions (the beasts, not the claws). What they told me is amazing, funny, and PRETTY SCARY.

Ah, I sense you may be asking yourself, "Whaaat? How does Andy Seed talk to animals?" Good question.

Well, a few years ago, I was messing around with some coat hangers, a broken waffle maker, and half a sock when I accidentally invented a machine to translate animals' sounds into words! Yes, the tranimalator was born. This device allows me to speak to any creature on the planet. Handy!

NICE TO MEET YOU!

So here are my interviews with ten remarkable animals. They tell you all the things you want to know, I hope, and perhaps some surprising facts too. And if you're not satisfied with the answers, well, you can argue with the tiger!

# Interview with a
# Bengal Tiger

My first guest needs no introduction. So why am I writing one? She's big, she's striped, she's scary, and she is here, all the way from the jungles and grasslands of India, to answer my questions. I am excited and TERRIFIED to bring you . . . a BENGAL TIGER!

**Q: Welcome. Uh, why do you have stripes?**
A: I tried spots, but they don't suit me, ha ha. No, it's really so I can hide in the long grass. How else do you think I'm going to sneak up on a deer, dear?

**Q: Do you enjoy hunting?**
A: Enjoy it? I LOVE it! Well, when I catch something I do. I HATE it when they get away. All that pouncing for nothing . . .

**Q: What's your favorite food?**
A: Oooh, good question. Well, deer is yummy, but I do like a juicy wild pig. A nice young buffalo is a treat for the cubs too.

**Q: What are your top tiger tips for catching prey?**
A: Go slowly and silently. Stay hidden. Choose tall grass if possible. Keep low and approach from behind. Get close, then hit the turbo boost! Finally, grab with your claws and bite the neck. Works for me.

**Q: You mentioned cubs. Are you their mother?**
A: Well, I'm not their bus driver! Yes, I have three cubs, about four months old now and pretty big. They are ALWAYS hungry.

**Q: Do you take them hunting with you?**
A: I'm starting to. But they just want to play most of the time. With hunting they can talk the talk, but can they stalk the stalk? NO.

**Q: Where are they?**
A: Back at our secret den among rocks, where they're safe. When they're born, they are tiny little helpless things.

**FAVORITE FOODS:**
Deer   Wild pig
Antelope   Water buffalo

**WORST ENEMIES:**
Leopard
Wild dog   Monkey
Jackal
Vulture

**Q: So, where's the cubs' father?**
A: Oh, that lazy thing? He doesn't help raise the kids! He's probably gone off to fight another tiger and steal its territory. Huh, if he weren't bigger than me, I'd give him a paw on the jaw!

**Q: What do you mean by "stealing territory"?**
A: It means taking over another tiger's hunting patch. Each of us has a large area of land where we hunt—so there's enough food for each of us. If another tiger comes into my territory, I'll chase it off.

**Q: What is your ideal day?**
A: A lot of snoozing, maybe a dip in the river when it gets too hot, and then a big pile of raw meat and guts. I can eat 45 pounds in one sitting. Mmmmm.

**Q: Is there anything annoying about being a tiger?**
A: Yes. Monkeys. I CANNOT STAND monkeys!

**Q: Ooh, why is that?**
A: They watch you from the trees and then screech their horrible alarm calls when you come near so that the deer run away. However, I do like EATING monkeys.

**Q: Which animals are your rivals?**
A: Leopards, wolves, wild dogs, jackals, crocodiles, and vultures, mainly. Pests.

**Q: What about humans?**
A: Oh yes, you guys . . . the only animal we're really afraid of, with your guns and poaching and taking away our hunting grounds to build houses on. Grrrrr!

**Q: Why do poachers shoot you?**
A: Our skins and body parts are worth a lot of money, sadly. Some people think my bones make good medicine. They don't. It's why there aren't many tigers left. Twits.

**Q: What's your favorite band?**
A: Def Leppard.

# Interview with a Wolf

My next special guest loves to roam the great northern forests of Asia and North America. He has yellow eyes and 42 big teeth, and he's, um, pretty grumpy by the looks of things. I bring you . . . a WOLF!

**Q: First of all, do you howl at the moon?**
A: No. Don't be ridiculous. Do *you* howl at the moon?

**Q: Fair point. But why do you howl?**
A: Isn't it obvious? There are times when a yelp or a growl or a whimper won't do. We howl to keep in touch with the pack or maybe frighten off other wolves.

**Q: You mentioned a pack. What's that?**
A: Sheesh, don't you know anything? It's a kind of extended family group. We work together to hunt and patrol our territory and defend each other.

**Q: What kinds of animals do wolves hunt?**
A: The bigger the better—more to eat. Deer are good, or caribou or elk. Or bison. Or beavers. Or musk oxen. Yum.

**Q: So how exactly do you deal with an animal that's bigger than you?**
A: Weren't you listening? We work as a pack. Chase it, tire it out, separate it from others, bite it, injure it, and then drag it down. Teamwork.

**Q: Do you eat just the meat?**
A: No.

**Q: Uh, can you tell me why?**
A: All right, I suppose so . . . Well, it would be a waste to only eat the meat, wouldn't it? We chomp almost everything: skin, guts, lungs, bones. You name it! I can eat 33 pounds in one go. Wolf it down! You can't waste food as a predator—it might be days or even weeks until you catch something again, especially in the hard northern winter. We can't go to the grocery store like you can!

DAD, WE'RE STUCK.

**Q: Wow, eating everything—that's impressive! How do you eat bones?**
A: Easy, we have a VERY powerful bite. We crush them and slurp the juicy marrow inside. You can test my bite if you'd like —give me your hand.

**Q: NO WAY! I believe you. But why is it that humans are so scared of wolves? You're the bad guy in LOTS of fairy tales.**
A: You're scared of *us*? That's hilarious. We're scared of *you*. And it's no wonder—over the centuries, people have hunted and killed wolves everywhere!

**Q: So why are people scared of you?**
A: Do I have to spell it out? Really? Okay, I can see that I do . . . Humans in the past cut down forests in our territories, wiped out our prey, and took our land for farming. We went hungry. So we ate some of their sheep and cattle. It was that or starve.

**Q: Are there any animals you don't get along with?**
A: Hmph, thought you might apologize for a minute there. Other animals? Hungry bears sometimes take our cubs or steal our food. So we bite them on the butt.

**Q: What are wolves good at?**
A: Tennis. No, not really. Running, swimming, keeping warm, raising cubs. We have great senses of smell and hearing too— way better than yours.

**Q: Is there anything that's not good about being a wolf?**
A: Sure, we hate interviews. And being the villain in books and movies. Okay, I can see you want a serious answer. Yes, we are often hungry, and we don't live very long— maybe seven years? Oh, this is depressing . . .

# Interview with a Giant Anteater

For my third interview, I am speaking to a hairy, handsome creature from Brazil. He's a big, bushy eater of bugs—I bring you the one and only GIANT ANTEATER!

**Q: What's it like to eat ants?**
A: It's cool, man—they're tastier than you think.

**Q: Do you eat anything else?**
A: Sure, we really go for termites too. Nom-nom-nom. They're like ants, but with a little more creamy goodness.

**Q: Don't termites live inside those big clay mounds? How do you get them out?**
A: It's no big deal, dude. We just bash a hole with our big claws, stick our beautiful snouts in, and lick up those tiny guys.

**Q: Is that easy to do?**
A: Yeah, easy. I have a two-foot-long tongue covered in sticky spit, man. I flick it in and out faster than you can blink, oh yeah.

**HOW TO EAT ANTS**
1. Sniff out a nest
2. Bash it with your claws
3. Stick your snout in
4. Lick 'em up
5. Get out of there!

**Q: But don't the ants bite you?**
A: You know it, bro! I am king of the sting. The secret is to just chow a few hundred before the bad-boy soldier ants come out to defend the colony. We don't mess with those dudes . . .

**Q: You're a big animal, so how do you survive on teeny little insects?**
A: Ha, they all ask that. If you only get two cornflakes for breakfast, you go back for more, don't ya? Well, I visit a lot of nests—maybe 150 a day. Adds up to about 35,000 insects. That's good eating, I'd say.

**Q: Your claws are huge—about four inches long. Are they only for digging out food?**
A: Hey, I am a brother of peace, you know. But there are some mean hunters in the jungle here. Big cats. Jaguars and cougars. If they mess with me, I am going to splash the slash, you know.

**Q: Where do you sleep?**
A: Ah, I love to snooze, man. I make a little hollow among shrubs or long grass and curl up under this big bushy blanket of a tail. Nice.

**Q: Um, you have a very long nose but a tiny mouth. Why's that?**
A: I know, I'm beautiful, aren't I? The long schnoz is to reach into ants' nests for grub, or grubs really, and the small mouth is because I don't need teeth for tiny termites.

**Q: You have no teeth?**
A: That's right, dude. No teeth and bad eyes, but I got an awesome sense of smell for sniffing out lunch.

**Q: Do you have children?**
A: Maybe. Probably. Uh, we dudes sort of live alone, you know. The females care for the kids. The little ones ride around on their backs. It's sweet.

**Q: Finally, what do you love and hate about being a giant anteater?**
A: Man, I really don't like wildfires, poachers, or humans that take our land. But give me a grassy plain full of fat creepy-crawlies, and I'm as happy as the stars in the sky. Peace!

# Interview with a
# Honey Badger

My next guest is smaller than you might think. She's about the size of a little dog and isn't really a badger. But she is tough, fearless, and nearly earless: come and meet the African HONEY BADGER!

**Q: Are you really as ferocious as everyone says?**
A: No, no, no, I'm as sweet as a little teddy bear, really. I wouldn't hurt a fly. Oh, and you'd better put that in the interview or I'll bite your nose off.

**Q: Gulp, uh, how much do you like honey?**
A: How much do *you* like chocolate ice cream? I don't just like it, I LOVE it. I looove it, I . . . well, you get the picture. Actually, I like munching the bee grubs in the nest too.

**Q: Don't the bees sting you when you smash open their nest?**
A: Yeah, whatever. I have very thick skin and tough fur.

**Q: What else do you like to eat?**
A: Whaddya got? I go for insects, lizards, birds, frogs, mice, gerbils, turtles, snakes, scorpions, eggs, and a few berries and roots now and then.

**Q: Snakes? Venomous ones?**
A: They're tasty. Sure, they bite me sometimes, but I just kill 'em and sleep it off. My body can tolerate the poison. Then I wake up and eat them. Bones and all. Delish.

**HOW TO HELP YOURSELF TO HONEY**
1. Sniff out a bees' nest
2. Climb the tree
3. Tear open the nest with claws
4. Get stung a few times
5. Eat the sweet stuff
6. Run!

**Q: Do you have many friends?**
A: If I did, I would only eat them . . . Ha ha, just kidding. No, honey badgers don't have friends—plenty of enemies, though. I prefer to be alone.

**Q: So if you don't like company, how do you keep other honey badgers away?**
A: By stink. It's all about the poop. And the pee. I leave piles of doo-doo around and I pee on trees and bushes. It's called scent marking. When others sniff it, they know to keep WELL away. I don't want them grabbing my grub.

**Q: Your claws are really long. Why's that?**
A: I dig with 'em, of course! Can't use a shovel! I can dig out larvae in the ground, make myself a burrow a yard or two deep, rip a bees' nest apart, and poke a hyena in the eye if it's annoying me. So now you know.

**Q: What are you good at?**
A: Well, digging I've told you about. Also biting. Plus fighting, killing, climbing, escaping from zoos, and surviving in a hot country full of dangers. I'm pretty awesome, come to think of it!

I'M GOING TO BITE YOU.

**Q: Anything you're not so good at?**
A: My sense of smell is FAB, but my hearing and eyesight are terrible. I mean, for all I can see, I could be talking to a lamp post right now . . .

**Q: If you're so great, why don't farmers like you?**
A: I don't like them! No, well, it's maybe, probably because we do, sort of, um, occasionally . . . kill a bunch of their chickens. But their fences are so easy to climb or dig under, and we can bite through wooden buildings. It's too easy. They're practically *asking* us to eat them.

**Q: Are there any animals you fear?**
A: Not really. I mean, I prefer not to be bitten by crocodiles or lions, but my skin is so thick that they often can't injure me anyway. I usually just ignore them.

**Q: Thanks. Is there anything else you'd like to tell me?**
A: Yes, I'm going now. Outta my way!

I'M GOING TO BITE *YOU*. A LOT.

# Interview with a Jaguar

Now a rare and beautiful beast joins us all the way from the wetlands of Mexico. He's a mean, muscly, menacing cat (or should that be car?). I bring you . . . a JAGUAR!

**Q: Can you tell me three interesting things about yourself?**
A: I suppose so, if I must . . . Let's see . . . First of all, I am not a kind of leopard. They're found in Africa and Asia, while we jaguars live in the Americas. Second, I am the third-biggest cat, after the tiger and lion. And finally, I'm a good swimmer.

**Q: What's it like to be a jaguar?**
A: How tiresome . . . I mean, good question! It's not easy. We don't have any predators, but we have to catch all our own food, and most of it is very good at running away. It's easy for plant eaters, but when you're a hunter, your next meal might be days away.

**Q: What are your spots for?**
A: You mean rosettes. Well, they help me hide among the leafy undergrowth so I can jump on passing pigs and other tasty creatures.

**Q: What is your favorite food?**

A: Ah, now you're talking! Wild boars are good and meaty, but I do love to sink my teeth into capybara—they taste so much better than anteaters. Deer are okay, armadillos make a nice snack, and an occasional turtle or fish adds variety.

**Q: What's the hardest thing to catch?**

A: Around here, a bus! No, but seriously, peccaries are fast and have a pretty nasty bite, and caimans are so slippery in the water. But I like a challenge.

**Q: Caimans are like crocodiles, aren't they? How do you catch them?**

A: More like small alligators, really. If you must know, I wait patiently on the riverbank until one comes close, and then I leap into the water and bite its head. I have to crack the skull, actually.

**Q: You can crack a skull?!**

A: Of course. Caimans are hard to kill, but I am rather strong. A powerful bite in the right place does the trick. Anyway, the caiman will bite me if I don't bite it first. *Yawn.* What else do you want to know?

**Q: Um, are you as fast as the other big cats?**

A: I'm more of an ambush hunter than a chaser. I'm an expert at stalking during dusk—creeping up, oh so quietly. It's all about stealth. Sure, I can dart forward and pounce at speed, but I'm not really a runner—too brawny.

**Q: Do you spend time with other jaguars?**
A: Certainly not! We defend our hunting territories at all costs. I roar to keep others away, and I leave droppings and urine markers too. We're each king of our own big stretch of forest or swamp.

**Q: Do you know any black panthers?**
A: No, but I've seen them. They're jaguars with very dark coats. Annoyingly good nighttime camouflage . . . but poachers seek them out, sadly.

**Q: Ranchers farm the land near where you live. Do you ever eat their cattle?**
A: Only if I am desperate for food. I usually stay away from humans. They cut down the trees and destroy everything. You seem all right, even if you do ask too many questions. Goodbye.

# Interview with a
# Polar Bear

Joining me now, straight from the far north, is the biggest, whitest land carnivore in the world. She's queen of the ice, marauder of the seas, and she knows her snow.
Yes, I bring you . . . a POLAR BEAR!

**Q: What is your dream?**
A: To be as fat as possible.

**Q: Whaaat! Most humans try to avoid becoming very large.**
A: Hmmm? Oh, yes, well, that's because you have too much food and we don't have enough.

**Q: Have you ever met a penguin?**
A: A what?

**Q: I'll take that as a no. They're South Pole creatures and you're North Pole, correct?**
A: Yes, but do you have any food? A nice baby whale perhaps?

**Q: Uh, sorry, not on this occasion. So what is your favorite time of year?**
A: Not the summer. I hate the summer.

**Q: Why's that?**
A: The sea ice melts! It's hard to get food! I have to go onto land and search around for tiny scraps like birds' eggs and seaweed.

**Q: What's winter like in the Arctic?**
A: Ludicrously cold, but my thick body fat keeps me warm. I don't like snowstorms because I can't see to hunt, and it's hard to sniff out seals when the wind is howling.

**Q: I notice you have enormous feet—why's that?**
A: *Yawn.* Sorry, I'm tired from walking for miles looking for something to eat. My feet? Wide paws are good for swimming and stop me from falling through the ice. And my claws help me grip. It's slippery stuff, you know.

**Q: Is it true that your skin is black?**
A: Yes. But our see-through fur looks white to help us sneak up on prey in the snow.

**Q: What are your best hunting skills?**
A: Okay, now you're talking. We live by the ocean because we depend on seals to eat. So we need frozen sea ice to get near our prey. We sniff them out from miles away, find their breathing holes in the ice, and then creep up and grab them when they surface. Dinner!

**Q: Why do you like seals so much?**
A: It's all about the blubber, brother—the fat. They are covered in lots of it to keep warm, and we eat it. It gives us the energy to survive.

I'VE HAD ENOUGH OF DANCING ON ICE!

**Q: So if you're good at hunting, why are you always hungry?**
A: Well, Mr. Interviewer, seals are very hard to catch. Most of the time they get away. But also the sea ice is melting— it seems like there's less of it every year. We have to swim several miles to reach it sometimes, and that really tires us out. I've known bears who have starved to death.

**Q: That's terrible. We humans keep warming the planet by polluting it. Have you heard of global warming?**
A: So it's YOU! I should eat you right now! Not much blubber on you, though . . . I prefer A SEAL to A SEED.

**Q: Sorry, we are trying to do something to stop climate change. It's not easy, though. Um, what else is hard about being a polar bear?**
A: Hmmm? Oh. Females like me sometimes go six months without eating. And then male bears sometimes kill our cubs. Wolves are a pain too, and being stabbed by a walrus tusk REALLY hurts.

**Q: Ouch. And what are the best things about being you?**
A: We're tough. Our sense of smell is amazing. We're epic swimmers. We can survive extreme cold, and we're not afraid of anything. And now, *yawn*, I must, uh, must . . . ZZZZZ . . .

# Interview with a Lion

If you can hear a roar, it's because I have a formidable creature with me right now. She's the pride of her pride, the queen of beasts, the mighty claw, coming to you straight from the wide plains of Africa. It's. The. One. And. Only. LION!

**Q: Have you ever seen *The Lion King*?**
A: Who's he? I thought I knew all the fellows around here.

**Q: It's a movie.**
A: Oh, in that case, no. Lions are not generally welcome in movie theaters.

**Q: What makes lions different from other big cats?**
A: Come on, it's obvious! We're the BEST for a start. We're noble, powerful, brave, handsome, and, uh, modest.

**Q: I thought you were different because you live in groups. Am I right?**
A: Well, yes, that's true. We live in family groups called prides—mine has 12 lions: two males, three females including me, and eight young ones.

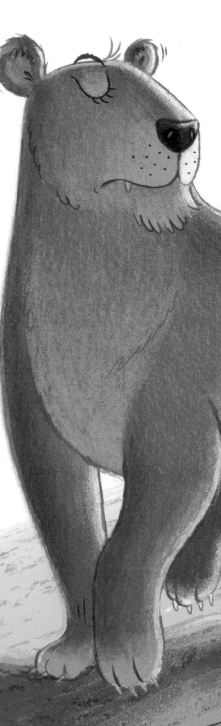

**Q: Doesn't that add up to 13?**
A: Hey, we're good at hunting, not math.

**Q: Okay, sorry. So why are lions called the "king of the jungle"?**
A: I have NO IDEA. We live in grasslands and open spaces, not forests. But we do like to be THE BOSS.

**Q: Have you ever had a fight with an elephant?**
A: Maybe. I'm not telling you who won . . . If we can't find a wildebeest or zebra to eat, we do sometimes try to grab baby elephants. But, yes, I SUPPOSE the adults are too big and strong for us, even though we are, you know, THE GREATEST.

**Q: What else do you hunt?**
A: Buffalo, big antelope, warthogs. Giraffes and hippos are annoyingly dangerous, and other things are mainly too small to feed the pride. We kill and eat or we die—there are NO RESTAURANTS FOR LIONS.

HOW TO HAVE ZEBRA FOR LUNCH
1. Spread out
2. Approach from different directions, staying hidden
3. Sprint after a lone individual and aim for the head
4. Everyone joins in to prevent escape
5. Bite the throat to crush windpipe
6. Feast!

**Q: How do you overcome a buffalo that's much larger and heavier than you?**

A: With skill and cunning, of course! And teamwork. We females often work together—one of us sneaks up in the tall grass while another might hide among the bushes to spring on it. You've got to drag down those bad boys and bite them in the throat, which takes A LOT OF STRENGTH. And their horns cause brutal wounds. But once that big beast is dead, it can feed us all for DAYS. Mmmmm.

**Q: Do you have any babies?**

A: Yes, two sweet little cubs. They're three months old now and are bundles of TROUBLE. All they want to do is PLAY! What an easy life . . .

**Q: What are they like when they are born?**

A: Really small and blind and quite helpless. Their eyes open after a week, and they start to walk after three weeks—and then they just want milk ALL THE TIME. I need to keep them hidden as well.

**Q: Why's that?**
A: Hyenas and leopards might kill them while I'm out hunting. Buffalo will trample them given half a chance. So I keep moving them.

**Q: What are the other dangers that lions face?**
A: Starvation. Even though we are AWESOME, most of our hunts fail. Human hunters also shoot us or use our territories for grazing cattle. Diseases often cause death too. LIFE IS HARD.

**Q: What do you think of male lions?**
A: Well, they're big and strong but basically LAZY as ANYTHING. We females do all the child-rearing and most of the hunting, and we take care of the pride. They just go off and get into fights. HMPH.

**Q: Thanks. Do you want to say anything else?**
A: Did I tell you that lions are THE BEST?

# Interview with a
# Giant Armadillo

For this interview, I welcome another mysterious mammal of South America. It's the mega-rare, solitary, and shy GIANT ARMADILLO!

**Q: Not many people have ever seen a giant armadillo. Why's that?**

A: Hello, very nice to meet you. Um, to answer your question, there aren't many of us around these days, and we prefer to live far away from human beings. Also we tend to sleep all day, out of sight.

**Q: Where do you sleep?**

A: Well, we snooze underground in special burrows, you see. We dig a new one every few days and then move on.

**Q: Wow! I'd hate to move to a new house twice a week—why don't you stay in the same burrow?**

A: Good question, well asked. We like to move around in search of food. We're picky eaters, rather.

**Q: What, you mean you only eat hamburgers and fries?**

A: Oh dear me, no, no, no—although some of our food does run away pretty quickly, so you could call it fast food. We feed on termites and ants, you see.

**Q: I notice that you have ENORMOUS claws—the big ones must be eight inches long. How do you grab tiny ants with those monsters?**

A: Ah, most excellent question, sort of. Our claws are for breaking into big hard termite mounds, so we can lick up the little insects. We also use them to dig our burrows.

**Q: Um, how do you find termite nests if you only come out at night?**

A: A very good point once again. Our eyesight is tragically feeble but we can smell remarkably well, so we follow our noses.

DIGGING IN PROGRESS

**Q: Right, I get it. You're also covered in hard scales, I see. Is that because you're always bumping into trees in the dark?**
A: Hehehe, oh no. These bony plates are for protection against beasts. There are hungry cougars and jaguars around, after all.

**Q: Are big cats your main problem?**
A: Oh, hmmm, how embarrassing . . . This really is most awkward . . . No, um, our main problem is a two-legged nincompoop.

**Q: What, chickens?**
A: Uh, no. I'm referring to the, um, human being.

**Q: Whoops, sorry. What have we done to you?**
A: Oh, not much really—just hunted us, eaten us, run over us with trucks, shot us as farm pests, and destroyed our habitats. Besides that, you've been great!

**Q: Yikes! Sorry about that. Quick change of subject . . .
You're called a giant armadillo—how big are you?**
A: Only three feet long or so. Not enormous, but bigger than any other armadillo, and that's what counts.

**Q: Those burrows you dig must be huge. Are they?**
A: Pretty big, yes. And because we keep making new ones, lots of other animals use them too—foxes, snakes, lizards, and more. We offer free housing for the homeless!

**Q: How kind and noble. Finally, do you have any good giant armadillo facts you'd like to share?**
A: Of course, with pleasure! We have 100 teeth; many local people call us tatú; and we detest being cold! See you later, and best wishes with your book—but tell your readers not to eat me, please.

# Interview with a Snow Leopard

My next clawed beast is a mysterious and beautiful big cat found in remote lands. It's a real honor to meet one of the rarest creatures on Earth—the fabulous SNOW LEOPARD.

**Q: Where exactly do you live?**
A: I'm currently residing among the western ridges of the Mongolian Plateau.

**Q: Say what?**
A: In the mountains of Asia.

**Q: Oh, right. What's it like there?**
A: It's a barren, desiccated landscape, featuring the extreme low temperatures and reduced oxygen levels associated with high altitudes of 10,000–16,000 feet.

**Q: Pardon?**
A: It's rocky and cold.

**Q: Why did you mention oxygen?**
A: The air is thin in my high habitat, so it's difficult to breathe. Well, it would be for you. I'm suited to it.

**Q: So what is a leopard doing in the snow?**
A: Surviving, hunting, reproducing, and being elusive, mostly.

**HOW TO BEAT THE COLD**
- Small, furry ears
- Extra-thick fur
- Very long, bushy tail
- Hairy pads on feet
- Big nostrils to heat freezing air

**Q: What does "elusive" mean?**

A: We are very rarely seen. Some people call us ghost cats. But it's principally because we live in steep, inaccessible areas where prey is scarce. Plus, we are low in number and spread out over a vast region. Our camouflage is highly developed too.

**Q: Don't you get really cold?**

A: Yes, but we are well adapted for survival—we have very dense fur, small ears to reduce heat loss, a long bushy tail to act as a blanket, and broad feet for walking on soft snow.

**Q: You're a hunter, you said—what do you eat?**
A: Mainly bharal, tahr, and ibex.

**Q: What?!**
A: Mountain sheep and goats.

**Q: Oh, right. Those things are amazing climbers. How do you catch them?**
A: Our rosettes and coloring enable us to hide effectively when stalking. We ambush from above on steep inclines, using speed to pursue, claws to grip, and teeth for the kill.

**Q: So you chase them down hills?**
A: Correct. And cliffs. We have exceptional balance.

**Q: A lot of clawed animals dislike humans. Do you hate us too?**
A: That's an interesting question. Poaching and herding have reduced our numbers considerably, and climate change is a danger, but the more enlightened humans have established national parks, wildlife sanctuaries, and nature reserves where we are protected.

**Q: So, um, some good, some bad?**
A: Exactly.

STEP 3: HIT THE SNOW!

40

STEP 2: OFF WE GO.

STEP 1: CROUCH DOWN LOW.

**Q: Can you roar?**
A: No, but I am capable of loud yowling when I wish to attract a mate.

**Q: Uh, do you know any jokes?**
A: An eagle told me one: Why are snow leopards no good at hide-and-seek? Because they're always spotted. It's not funny.

**Q: Ha ha, I liked it! Finally, do you enjoy being one of the planet's rarest animals?**
A: Some say I am the Guardian of the Heavenly Peaks. Others call me the Lord of the Rocks that Reach the Sky, or Mystic Spirit of Ice. But I am merely a shy cat. This interview is over.

**Q: Ooh, well, thank you.**
A: Farewell.

# Interview with a
# Three-toed Sloth

My final interview is with one of planet Earth's strangest animals. He may be slow in body, but he's certainly not slow in mind. Let me introduce the cheery, sassy SLOTH!

**Q: First of all, where exactly do sloths live?**
A: 1601 Plum Street, Kansas City, Missouri.

**Q: Really?**
A: No, of course not! Really we live in trees. I'm from the rain forests of Costa Rica, in Central America. Hi!

**Q: Uh, hi. Now, everyone knows that sloths move very slowly—is it because you're lazy?**
A: Whatever.

**Q: Excuse me?**
A: Sorry, just kidding! I do a lot of that. Lazy, you ask? No, we are not. It's just that we need to save energy because our diet is poor. We only eat leaves, and they aren't very substantial food.

**Q: I suppose that's a pretty good reason! Why is your fur green in places?**

A: It's because we can't afford tissues . . . *atchoo!* No, really it's algae growing on us. It's damp in the rain forest, see. But the algae is harmless—we're not going moldy. I hope!

**Q: Do you like being a sloth?**

A: It's better than being a piece of toast! Actually, I do like it, although life is just one big rush these days . . .

**Q: Your claws are impressive. Why are they so big?**

A: Big ones were on sale so . . . ha ha, joking! Actually, they're big 'cause we use them for climbing, which is very important when you live in trees. And they're a good defense against naughty rival sloths too.

**Q: Who are your deadliest enemies?**

A: The Joker, Magneto, and Lex Luthor. Just kidding again— ha, I can't help it. In truth, it's jaguars, big snakes, and harpy eagles, because they have this annoying habit of eating us now and then. I can't believe you interviewed a jaguar for this book as well . . . I bet he didn't say sorry.

**Q: Whoops, quickly moving on . . . Um, why do some sloths squeak really loudly?**

A: Why not? Actually, those are females who are ready to have a baby. They screech to attract a mate. Whispering gets you nowhere in the jungle.

**Q: So sloths don't live in groups?**

A: Yes, I'm in a rock band. JK! No, we're solitary animals—which means we live alone.

**Q: If you could change three things about yourself, what would they be?**

A: Okay, no jokes this time. First, I would like to be able to call Greta Thunberg and ask her to stop loggers from cutting down our forest for wood. Second, I'd like better eyesight—I can hardly see my own butt! And third, I would like bigger muscles. As it is, a marathon would take me a week. Really.

**Q: Hmm, interesting. Finally, can you tell everyone your favorite sloth facts please?**
A: One, we hate facts. Not really!
We LOVE facts. Okay, here goes:

1. Sloths are good at swimming.
2. We can hold our breath for 40 minutes.
3. We only poop once a week. We climb down to the forest floor, make a hole, and do it there. But . . . our poops are HUGE! So now you know.

**Q: Super, uh, good. Thank you, Mr. Sloth.**
A: It's been a total nightmare—I mean pleasure. Ha ha!

# How you can help

I hope you enjoyed meeting the animals in this book. I did, even if some of them scared me a little. But I am worried that I might NEVER SEE some of them again.

Several of the clawed beasts in this book are ENDANGERED. That has the word DANGER in it. It's bad. It means they might be gone forever, like the poor dead dodo bird, if we don't help protect them by taking care of our planet.

Here are some ways you can help make sure that tigers, polar bears, and giant anteaters are still around when you are all big and old.

## 1. Get active

It helps to understand what the wild outdoors is like.
So ask for a trip to the country:
- Walk in the woods—go bird watching
- Climb a big hill
- Explore a mountain if you have one nearby
- Follow a stream—stick to the trail!

## 2. Join a local group

There are groups of people everywhere who work to care for the environment. Many organizations that protect animals offer activities and clubs for children, such as your local Audubon Society.

## 3. "Bee" a gardener

If you are lucky enough to have a backyard, here are some ways to encourage wildlife:
- Plant flowers to encourage important insects, such as bees
- Start a compost pile—the best way to naturally recycle kitchen and garden waste. Creepy-crawlies love compost piles!
- Grow some vegetables, such as potatoes or tomatoes—you'll find they taste amazing, yum!
- Plant a small tree

## 4. Raise money

Nature organizations and big nonprofits like World Wildlife Fund (WWF) depend on money to do important conservation work, protecting the wildlife that is under threat. Here's how you can help them:

- Adopt an endangered animal with WWF or a similar group
- Ask a teacher if your school can help with raising money for wildlife
- Find out about smaller nonprofits that help animals, such as owls, bats or orangutans

## 5. Help prevent pollution

Making and using most things involves energy and can create nasty pollution. Transportation adds to climate change too, and all of this affects wild animals. Here are some ways to REDUCE pollution:

- Turn off lights when you're not using them
- Unplug chargers
- Switch off devices when you're finished with them
- Walk or bike short distances instead of going by car
- Reuse and recycle as much as possible
- Don't litter

## 6. Avoid using plastic

We now know that tiny pieces of plastic are getting into oceans, rivers, soil, and more. This is not good for animals!

- Instead of plastic bags, use any bag that can be used several times
- For drinks, use a bottle that can be refilled
- Use bars of soap instead of shower gel in plastic bottles

## 7. Tell our leaders

It's up to the people in charge to make changes that help wildlife. You can encourage them by writing letters that show that you care about protecting wild animals and their habitats. Ask a parent or guardian how to do this.

## 8. Learn more

This book has helped you understand a little about the lives of some special animals. Use your local library (where the books are free to borrow) to find out more, and to discover what else you can do to protect OUR AMAZING PLANET.

# Quiz

Can you answer these ten sneaky questions about the animals in this book? All the information is on the pages somewhere! Answers are at the bottom of this page.

**1. Where are tiger cubs usually born?**
a) Up a tree
b) In a den
c) By a river
d) In the hospital

**2. What is a group of wolves called?**
a) A howl
b) Debbie
c) Team Bite
d) A pack

**3. How do giant anteaters eat ants?**
a) With a knife and fork
b) They lick them with a long, sticky tongue
c) By sucking them out
d) Using their special teeth

**4. Honey badgers keep their rivals away by leaving piles of what?**
a) Poop
b) Bones
c) Dull magazines
d) Honey

**5. Which of these is a favorite food of jaguars?**
a) Termites
b) Leopards
c) Toasted cheese
d) Wild boar

**6. How do polar bears find seals to eat?**
a) By swimming around
b) By climbing icebergs to spot them
c) By smell
d) By using an app called SealtheDeal

**7. How many teeth does a giant armadillo have?**
a) None
b) One huge one
c) 100
d) 14½

**8. Which of these things helps keep a snow leopard warm?**
a) Small ears
b) A big nose
c) Wide feet
d) A knitted hat

**9. Where do lions usually hunt for buffalo?**
a) In town
b) In the jungle
c) In pants
d) In long grass

**10. How big is a three-toed sloth's poop?**
a) Teeny-weeny
b) Medium-size
c) Huge
d) Bigger than a suitcase